About the author

Graham Gibbs is Head of the Oxford Centre For Staff Development, a network of staff development consultants and the largest provider of staff development to higher education in the UK. He was previously Head of the Educational Methods Unit at Oxford Polytechnic and Head of the Study Methods Research Group at the Open University. He is the author of many of the TES books in the '53 ...' series as well as *Learning by Doing*, *Teaching Students To Learn*, *Improving Student Learning* and *Coping with Large Classes*. He runs over 50 workshops a year on teaching and learning issues, including short courses on appraising teaching. He has acted as a consultant to institutions on designing appropriate mechanisms to appraise teaching and to reward excellent teaching.

Books by Technical and Educational Services

53 Interesting Things To Do In Your Lectures

53 Interesting Things To Do In Your Seminars And Tutorials

53 Interesting Ways To Assess Your Students

53 Interesting Ways Of Helping Your Students To Study

53 Interesting Communication Exercises For Science Students

53 Interesting Ways To Appraise Your Teaching

53 Interesting Ways To Promote Equal Opportunities In Education

53 Interesting Ways To Teach Mathematics

53 Interesting Ways To Write Open Learning Materials

253 Ideas For Your Teaching

Interesting Ways To Teach: Seven Do-It-Yourself Training Exercises

Preparing To Teach: *An Introduction To Effective Teaching In Higher Education*

Getting the Most From Your Data: *Practical Ideas On How To Analyse Qualitative Data*

Contents

Acknowledgement

This guide was inspired by and modelled on the *'Guide to the teaching dossier: its preparation and use'* prepared by the Teaching Effectiveness Committee of the Association of University Teachers of Canada, with the help of the Centre for Teaching and Learning Services, McGill University. Their work is gratefully acknowledged.

Preface

Lecturers in further and higher education are beginning to find that the quality their teaching is being judged by others. Many lecturers are used to students completing confidential course evaluation questionnaires. Many lecturers, especially in public sector higher education, are used to formal, and relatively impersonal, course reviews. But teachers are now finding that they are facing promotion panels where their teaching is closely scrutinised. They are facing annual appraisal interviews where the quality of their teaching is discussed. They are finding that when they apply for and are interviewed for teaching posts they are asked about their competence as teachers.

There are long-standing conventions as to how to present information about academic qualifications, research, publications, scholarship and administrative experience. It is not difficult to prepare a curriculum vitae or an application for promotion along these lines. However there are few such conventions about how to present information about excellence in teaching. This problem is not confined to lecturers who need a succinct way to portray their quality as teachers to others. Those making the judgements are also in trouble. They are being expected to make important decisions on the basis of inadequate information.

This book addresses this problem. It provides clear guidelines for preparing evidence about teaching for the purpose of judgement of the quality of that teaching by others, whether for promotion, appraisal or appointment.

It is based on a decade of practical experience in Britain and in Canada. In particular it is based on the experience of the promotion system at Oxford Polytechnic. For years the first criterion for promotion to Principal Lecturer had been concerned with excellence in teaching. And for years this criterion had not been able to be implemented because Senior Lecturers did not know how to present convincing and succinct evidence about their own teaching. The promotions panel had wanted to take teaching more seriously but did not have sufficient confidence in the poor evidence in front of them to make decisions based on teaching excellence. The introduction of the use of teaching profiles, and years of experience working with individual lecturers to put profiles together, helped to change this situation. Lecturers who were primarily excellent as teachers started being promoted. Lecturers who were excellent researchers but who presented unconvincing information about their teaching were less likely to get promoted. The reward system and the values of the institution changed.

Since the publication of the first edition of this book the use of teaching profiles has spread widely in the USA and Australasia and a number of publications are now available to support these developments.

I recommend that this guide is adopted as part of promotion, appraisal and appointment procedures in every department and institution where the quality of teaching is taken seriously.

Graham Gibbs
August, 1991.

Introduction

What is a teaching profile?

A teaching profile is a document you create which pulls together evidence about your competence as a teacher. It is used to present an overall picture of your teaching to others in a concise and convincing way.

What is a teaching profile for?

Teaching profiles can be used to present evidence about yourself when you apply for promotion. While there are conventions about how to present information about your publication and research record, there are few conventions about how to present your teaching record. A teaching profile fills that gap.

A teaching profile can also be used in preparation for an appraisal interview. It allows you to provide your appraiser with supporting evidence, to be read before the interview, to which you can both refer should questions be raised about your competence.

A brief teaching profile can also be used as part of a c.v. when you apply for teaching jobs.

What could a teaching profile contain?

This guide suggests 32 categories of evidence. It describes each category, explains the rationale for each category, and gives a concrete example of what each might look like. These examples are set in the context of an imaginary Egyptology course! The categories are divided into six groups:

- **Educational aims and objectives**
  What are you trying to achieve in your teaching?

- **Teaching methods**
  How do you go about your teaching? What special methods have you introduced?

- **Assessment**
  How do you assess your students, and how do you give them feedback on what they have learned? How do you know that your assessment methods are effective?

- **Evidence of the outcomes of teaching**
  What have your students learned? What have they achieved and what are they able to go on and do?

- **Evaluation evidence**
  How do you monitor and evaluate your courses and collect student feedback? What does this evaluation evidence tell you about your teaching?

- **Evidence of the continued study of teaching and learning**
  What do you do to improve your own teaching and that of your discipline and institution? What courses have you attended on teaching and what have you written about teaching?

How to create a teaching profile

- **Plan ahead**
  It can be difficult to put together a convincing teaching profile without having planned to do so, because it requires the collection of documentation over time. Just as it is necessary to keep an up-to-date list of your publications, a record of your research grants and so on, so it is necessary to keep a dossier on your teaching including, for example, course evaluation evidence. You may not be in the habit of keeping evidence about your teaching so it may be useful to open a file and start now. Get into the habit of putting everyday information into your teaching dossier: you can select items from it later.

- **Use existing material**
  A teaching profile is ideally a selection from an existing dossier rather than a specially written document. It should contain documents created for other purposes, such as routine student feedback on your courses, exam papers and results and teaching materials you have prepared. Putting it together shouldn't take a lot of effort if you have planned ahead.

- **Pay attention to local criteria**
  While this guide suggests 32 categories of information which you might include in your teaching profile, not all of these will be relevant (or even credible) in your own department or institution. Whether your teaching profile is being used for appraisal, for promotion, or for other purposes, there are likely to be local criteria concerning what really counts as good teaching, and what counts as evidence about good teaching. Make sure you find out what these criteria are, and select items for your profile accordingly.

- **Keep it short**
  Neither Heads of Department undertaking their twentieth appraisal interview, nor promotion panels sifting through the hundredth application, are usually prepared to spend long inspecting and interpreting the fine details of the evidence in front of them. You will have to make an impact quickly and

succinctly. Be very selective about your profile, choosing items which highlight your strengths and achievements and which your readers will find convincing. Refer your reader to appendices if you want to include detailed evidence such as student feedback or an example of teaching material. Keep the profile itself short.

- **Present it professionally**
  Make your profile look presentable. Provide a clear contents list with clearly labelled appendices. Highlight the main points, present material neatly and put it together in a smart folder.

Suggested contents of a teaching profile:

Educational aims and objectives

Teaching methods

Assessment methods

Evidence of outcomes of teaching

Evaluation evidence

Evidence of the continued study of teaching and learning

Educational aims and objectives

1 Course objectives

The purpose of including aims and objectives is that it can be difficult to judge the appropriateness or quality of teaching and of learning outcomes without first being clear what a course is supposed to achieve.

Aims and objectives can be evaluated on their own. For example are they consistent with aims of the course or degree programme as a whole? And are they at an appropriate educational level given the level or year of the course? Are they sufficiently clear and well formulated to aid course design and guide assessment, or are they nebulous and unhelpful?

However aims and objectives are more important as a framework within which course design, teaching methods, assessment methods and learning outcomes can be evaluated. The extent to which course aims, methods and measured outcomes are congruent provides indications about the overall quality of teaching.

Aims and objectives are not the same as syllabus listings. The purpose of stating them is not to indicate what subject matter will be 'covered', but rather to indicate what the outcome of 'covering' it should consist of. This can be stated in terms of what students should be able to do at the end of the course. For example students should perhaps be able to describe certain theories, solve certain problems, evaluate certain situations, design particular types of experiments, or whatever. The most crucial test of the adequacy of the way an objective is stated is whether its lack of achievement is testable (in the same way that a scientific theory should be refutable).

On some courses (for example B/TEC courses) the aims and objectives may have been formulated by others and are out of the direct control of the individual lecturer. It may still be worth stating such fixed objectives, however, in order to be able to appraise the ways in which they are reflected in teaching and assessment methods which are under the lecturer's control.

1 Course objectives

Description

A statement of the course objectives for courses or elements to which attention will be drawn in other items.

Rationale

Statements of carefully formulated objectives may show that care has been taken in course design. But the main purpose of stating course objectives is to provide a context for subsequent items so that evidence you present concerning teaching and assessment methods, evidence of student learning, and course evaluation evidence, can be interpreted in the light of these objectives.

Example

***Advanced Egyptological Methods** (999) has the aim, within **Ancient History**, of:*

a *providing students with the theoretical understanding and practical skills necessary to undertake independent research in the field of Egyptology, and*

b *contributing more generally to students' abilities to undertake historical studies.*

At the end of the course students will be able to:

1. *Describe the main research methods employed in Egyptology.*
2. *Undertake small-scale studies using both Fast and Slow methods.*
3. *Explain the theoretical basis for these methods.*
4. *Assess the appropriateness of the application of these methods to the study of selected issues in Egyptology.*

5 *Extract general principles and issues from Egyptological methods which have implications for the study of history in general.*

These objectives are directly associated with specific assessment methods (see 9 below).

Teaching methods

2 Range and level of teaching

3 Pattern of teaching methods used

4 Special teaching methods used

5 Course materials prepared for students

6 Use of special learning resources

7 Availability to students

8 Identification of special difficulties

2 Range and level of teaching

Description

A brief listing of the courses you have taught to indicate the range and level of your teaching, together with a very brief description of any special characteristics of those courses.

Rationale

Higher level courses may require more specialist subject knowledge, and introductory courses may require more teaching skill. A wide range of courses may make exceptional demands and require more varied teaching approaches. Particular student groups may pose special teaching problems. For example an introductory statistics course for social science students generally poses special challenges, as does a communication skills course for engineers.

Example

I am currently course leader on: 977 – ***Introduction to Egyptology****; 998 –* ***Origins of Egyptology****, and 999 –* ***Advanced Egyptological Methods****. While the same group of students tend to take all three courses, they have very varied concerns. About a third of them intend to become practising Egyptologists and two thirds have more general interests. These courses form a coherent, relatively discrete pathway.*

I also contribute to the teaching on: ***Archaeological Methods****, which involves workshops and practical field work trips in the second and third years; and on* ***Statistics for Egyptologists*** *which is a compulsory first year course.*

I am currently supervising eight third year projects/dissertations and one postgraduate in the final year of a PhD. I have successfully supervised six PhD students and five M.Sc. students through to completion since 1980.

3 Pattern of teaching methods

Description

List of methods used on particular course(s) and a description of the relationship between them. Statement as to how the choice of methods is intended to achieve the aims and objectives stated under the first heading.

Rationale

Variety of teaching methods and matching of methods to aims can indicate flexibility and adaptability in teaching and thoroughness in course design. Uniformity and a narrow range of methods, regardless of aims, can indicate limited skill, inflexibility, and an undifferentiated and unsophisticated approach to course design.

Example

Advanced Egyptological Methods *(999). Four introductory lectures (objective 1J; four tape-slide programmes and two videotapes demonstrating methods (objectives 1 and 2); three practical sessions for the practice of basic methods (objective 3) and two practical projects involving a choice of specialist applications (objective 4); individual literature reviews to survey use of methods (objective 4); group project to study relationship of Egyptological methods to Historical methods generally, followed by group tutorials (objective 5).*

4 Special teaching methods used

Description

Brief description of special method used, its purpose, and the extent of its use.

Rationale

Good teachers often develop a particular teaching method for a particular application or make a speciality of a technique, using it with skill and great effectiveness. This can provide evidence of the development and improvement of teaching, and of a particular aspect of excellence.

Example

*In **Advanced Egyptological Methods** (999) the conventional way of demonstrating techniques to students is in large groups in the laboratory. However it is time-consuming to set up such demonstrations, difficult to highlight all the key aspects of the method for many students at a time to see clearly and difficult to arrange practice for many students in parallel. I developed a series of tape-slide programmes to demonstrate the discrete stages of each method, and videotape programmes to show these stages in a 'live' sequence. The tapes are accompanied by a series of questions and students need to view and re-view the tapes until they can answer the questions. The students' ability to use these methods is then developed in independent-study practicals, which students can do as often as they feel they need to, in their own time. This independent-study way of demonstrating and gaining practice in the use of methods has now been adopted in other practical courses under my guidance. The tape-slide programmes have now been sold to four Egyptology Departments in other Institutions.*

5 Course materials prepared for students

Description

Course guides, learning packages, laboratory manuals, handouts, study guides, reading guides, etc. A copy of all materials is provided for each student.

Rationale

The preparation of such material is one indication of thoroughness and preparedness in teaching.

Example

I produced a set of extensive reading guides to help inexperienced students cope with difficult reading material on the course ***Introduction to Egyptology****. One such guide is attached as Appendix III.*

6 Use of special learning resources

Description

Film, videotape, computer-assisted learning package, audio tape, tape-slide, collection of maps or slides, or special equipment, etc., provided as learning resources, together with a description of how they are used.

Rationale

The provision of such material is one indication of preparedness for, and deliberate provision of variety in, teaching, especially when such materials have been produced by the teacher.

Example

I am jointly responsible, with A.B., for the establishment and stocking of a resources room for students, containing specimens, maps and slides and other non-book materials, to support practical courses in the department. Over 4,000 items had been catalogued by 01/07/88. These resources enable independent mini-projects to be undertaken by students. For example, resources are used to support independent study practicals on course 999.

7 Availability to students

Description

Statement of amount of time or schedule of time available to students outside of class, and perhaps of student use of this time, supported by appointment record.

Rationale

Some teaching is highly dependent on brief 'tutorial' encounters which are much less visible than formal teaching. Students greatly value the availability and approachability of staff.

Example

I keep 6 office hours a week clear for drop-in tutorials which are particularly important for the project and independent study modules. Appendix IV itemises the use of these hours in term 2 1988/89. I am also available to students during the use of laboratories for independent study practicals on course 999 (see 4 above) – 3 hours/week.

8 Identification of special difficulties

Description

Summary of steps taken to identify students with special problems or problems widely experienced, and of steps taken to deal with these problems.

Rationale

Few course designs, or teaching methods, solve all problems for all students. The diagnosis and cure of specific problems may identify the more perceptive and thorough teacher who undertakes additional tasks beyond the basic course description requirements.

Example

*On course 997 – **Introduction to Egyptology**, many students experience great difficulty with the somewhat daunting reading material (in the absence of a suitable basic text). Evaluation (see below) showed students to be reading little and gaining little from their reading). In 1986 I produced a series of reading guides (see 5 above) and since 1981 I have held two reading workshops at the start of each term. These workshops are now attended by students from other courses in the department. Evaluation has shown that the amount of reading they do has increased markedly.*

Assessment methods

9 Range of assessment methods

10 Provision of feedback to students

11 Reliability of assessment

9 Range of assessment methods

Description

Statement of variety of assessment methods used accompanied by a brief statement as to which educational aims are assessed by which methods. One particular course may be chosen to illustrate the pattern of methods employed. Examples may be appended, e.g. the exam paper.

Rationale

Despite varied educational aims and objectives, and varied teaching and learning methods, there is sometimes a uniformity of assessment methods which makes measurement of the attainment of all but a very narrow range of objectives unlikely. The use of varied assessment methods, carefully matched both to objectives and to the nature of student learning activities would tend to indicate thoroughness and differentiation in teaching and more careful course planning. Within the use of a particular assessment method, the specification of criteria, or use of marking schemes, may also indicate a more thorough approach.

Example

Advanced Egyptological Methods (999) (See course objectives listed above)

Objective 1 — *Describe the main methods employed in Egyptology.*
Assessed by: — *Two classroom administered MCQ tests (5% each) in weeks 2 and 4.*

Objective 2 — *Undertake small-scale studies using both Fast and Slow methods.*
Assessed by: — *Practicals (independent) on use of methods. Repeated use until successful. Pass/fail. (5% for each of 2 methods).*

Objective 4	*Assess the appropriateness of the application of these methods to the study of selected issues in Egyptology.*
Assessed by:	*Two practical projects. Project reports (20% each).*
Objective 3 and Objective 5	*Explain the theoretical basis for these methods.* *Extract general principles and issues from Egyptological methods which have implications for the study of history in general.*
Assessed by:	*Exam (paper attached as Appendix III). Two compulsory questions, one essay-type on the theoretical basis of methods, one on group project work (20% each).*

10 Provision of feedback to students

Description

Statement of methods used to provide students with information concerning their progress achieving objectives, and concerning remedial work necessary. Both formal and informal methods may be cited.

Rationale

At least some aspects of assessment should be formative rather than summative, i.e. to guide students rather than measure how far they have got. The variety, extent, quality and timing of feedback may all indicate excellence in teaching.

Example

Advanced Egyptological Methods (999) Student feedback is provided through:

- *a* *immediate knowledge of results in two MCQ tests*
- *b* *competence-based test of practical use of methods: repeated use until successful*
- *c* *structured feedback sheet on practical project reports (average 200 words/student report and grade, under five headings)*
- *d* *1 hour tutorial to discuss each group project*
- *e* *availability for individual tutorials during office hours (see 7 above)*
- *f* *peer feedback from co-operative group project work*

11 Reliability of assessment

Description

Brief statement of evidence of reliability of elements of assessment and of overall assessment.

Rationale

The end product of assessment grades is (usually) a single grade (e.g. a degree classification) which indicates how good a student is when compared with other students. A well-developed course assessment system will contribute to this differentiation of students, in the sense that students who do well on a particular course unit, or module, should also get a good degree. A module on which students who do badly also get a good degree may have problems with its assessment system. A teacher who can produce evidence of the reliability of his or her assessment methods is demonstrating a concern for the use to which grades are put.

Example

Coefficients of reliability (between students' overall module grade and degree classification)

Module 997 +.40 (Introductory module)
998 +.55
999 +.61

Correlation matrix for assessment elements in 999:

	MCQ Test	*Project*
Project	*+.52*	——
Exam	*+.65*	*+.61*

Evidence of the outcomes of teaching

12 Student grades

13 Products of student learning

14 Student publications, awards and exhibitions

15 Student progress to more advanced courses

16 External examiner's reports

12 Student grades

Description

Class average and/or distribution of grades, with an indication of the standard expected, e.g. in the light of past experience, grades in previous years or changes to the course.

Rationale

Student grades are influenced by factors beyond the teacher's control: by the quality of students, by externally applied standards, by the inherent difficulty of the course content, etc. Furthermore most grades are supposed to be 'distributed on a curve', giving much the same average and distribution regardless of the unit or module. Data under this heading should therefore be offered either when direct comparisons with past situations are possible, or when it is generally agreed that the course concerned confronts students with particular challenges unrelated to the teaching.

Example

In the first year compulsory unit, ***Statistics for Egyptologists****, 90% of the students have no mathematical background beyond 'O' level. Up to 1985 over 50% of the students failed this unit. Since I introduced new teaching methods, performance on this unit, using the same test, has consistently risen:*

1986/87 Term 1	*58% pass*
1986/87 Term 2	*60% pass*
1987/88 Term 1	*65% pass*
1987/88 Term 2	*71 % pass*

In 1988/89 all students passed the test, so that for the first time all 2nd year students now have a basic competence in statistics.

13 Products of student learning

Description

Note of exemplary work produced by student(s) and possibly with brief examples appended: laboratory work-books, supervised dissertations, artifacts, map work, essays, design, etc.

Rationale

Quality is sometimes best illustrated by looking at student products whose excellence cannot adequately be conveyed by grades. Such examples may be important where there may be concern that standards have been compromised, or that a competence-based or pass/fail approach might have brought a levelling-down of standards, or in general when an increase in quality has followed changes to a course.

Example

*In my **Engineering Drawing** classes the standards of drawing have remained consistently high despite falling levels of student ability on entry. This has been achieved by the introduction of remedial drawing workshops. Appendix VII contains four photocopies of (reduced) drawings representing grades of A, B+, B and C.*

14 Student publications, awards or exhibitions

Description

A short list or description of such accomplishments.

Rationale

Whilst factors beyond a teacher's control influence the quality of students' work, and internally judged standards may be questioned, accomplishments such as publication in a journal, an award or exhibition are seldom achieved without special encouragement and guidance at a high level.

Example

A student group project on ***Advanced Egyptological Methods*** *has been accepted for publication by the International Egyptology Review following the award of the 1988 Rameses prize for scholarship.*

15 Student progress to more advanced courses

Description

A sentence noting the numbers of students who progress on to a more advanced area of study.

Rationale

Student choice of the same subject for further study and success in gaining places to study at a higher level, may indicate both the level of interest aroused and the level of performance achieved by the teacher.

Example

60% of students studying 997 go on to 998. 80% of those studying 998 go on to 999. A high proportion of those successfully completing 999 go on to gain places to study Egyptology at postgraduate level: 14% in 1985/86, 18% in 1986/87 and 23% in 1987/88.

16 External examiners' reports

Description

Reference to statement(s) by external examiner(s) concerning the quality of student learning outcomes as evident in work viewed by them. Include examiners' statement, if short. Append if longer.

Rationale

Quality of learning outcomes is sometimes difficult for non-subject specialists to judge. External examiners' views carry special weight. Extracts from external examiners' reports may provide convincing evidence of excellence.

Example

In the external examiner's report on the Ancient History degree programme (1987/88) unit 998 and especially 999 were singled out for special mention:

"..

....

...."

Evaluation evidence

17 Course evaluation procedures

18 Course evaluation data

19 Evidence from student, department or institutional evaluation

20 Unsolicited written evidence

21 Action research

17 Course evaluation procedures

Description

Statement of steps taken to evaluate teaching.

Rationale

Both the use of routine procedures and particular investigations may indicate the degree of professionalism and care with which a teacher monitors, maintains and improves standards.

Example

997, 998 and 999 are evaluated every time they run. The method of evaluation varies according to the changes which have taken place and which issues I am currently focusing on. Appendix VIII contains two contrasting questionnaires used in 1986/87 and 1987/88. Students use a self-evaluation questionnaire to monitor their own seminar group behaviour in 998. I have used the educational development service to analyse qualitative data from 997 following a classroom discussion. I regularly invite colleagues in to 997 sessions, to get their views. I have acted as an 'external' evaluator for three of my colleagues on their courses: Dr X, Dr Y and Mr Z. I undertook a survey of Departments offering postgraduate Egyptology courses, museums and other employers of Egyptologists (a sample of 85 in all) inquiring about their expectations from undergraduates and about their view of our undergraduates.

Course evaluation procedures

18 Course evaluation data

Description

Summary of selected evidence concerning the quality of teaching and course design; fuller evidence appended.

Rationale

Student views of teaching are important evidence. Quantitative ratings should, wherever possible, be comparative. Many different forms of evidence might be offered. The evaluation instrument should be appended. Generalised statements such as 'students express satisfaction with my teaching' may carry little weight without more formally presented evidence.

Example

Appendix IX summarises student ratings on 997 for the years 1985/86, 1986/87 and 1987/88. As can be seen the only negative response has concerned workloads, and these ratings have improved following negotiation of staggered coursework deadlines with other course units. Appendix X shows data from the standard teacher evaluation questionnaire in relation to the average ratings for other lecturers in the Department who have used the same questionnaire. For the rating 'this lecturer in relation to others' I rate 4.2 (on a scale where 1=worst and 5=best) compared with an average of 3.4 for lecturers in the Department.

19 Evidence from student, department or institutional evaluations

Description

Summary of selected evidence; reference to appended fuller data if necessary.

Rationale

Evidence collected and collated by others, employing their criteria for excellence, may be more convincing than self-selected, self -administered and self-interpreted evaluation.

Example

The Departmental comparison of modules showed 997 and 998 to be high on both 'intellectual demand' and 'interest' and average on 'workload' (in relation to other modules). 998 was identified as 'amongst the best modules taken' by 50% of students taking it (ref. Departmental Board paper 88/17).

20 Unsolicited written evidence

Description

Summary of points made in written comments from others concerning teaching excellence.

Rationale

Students sometimes write to thank teachers for specific courses, after the completion of their studies, or following relevant employment. Colleagues may feel very positively about the teacher especially in the context of team teaching or if special assistance has been given. Written statements may be listed, summarised and/or appended.

Example

Three colleagues have closely observed the operation of the independent study practicals, which I use in 999. These are supported by tape-slide programmes and by other specially prepared learning materials in the resources room. I subsequently helped them to introduce similar elements into their course units. Appendix X is a written statement from these colleagues concerning this.

21 Action research

Description

Brief description of action research with emphasis on evidence of change and environment.

Rationale

Course evaluation and improvement activities are sometimes quite extensive and concentrate on a specific problem and innovation which is monitored in some detail. 'Action research' is a properly undertaken study of an aspect of one's own development activity. It may contain proper 'before and after' tests of student performance or allow other 'before and after' comparisons to be made.

Example

Students' performance on ***Statistics for Egyptologists*** *has always been a problem. I undertook with Dr W. a study of students' mathematical knowledge prior to the course, and reviewed and selected existing self-study elementary mathematical self-teaching materials, the best of which were then located in the Resources Room. Students entering the module are given a diagnostic test of mathematical ability, informed of the gap between their ability and the prerequisites of the Unit, and pointed towards appropriate self-study materials. Dr S. acts as a tutor, on a surgery basis, to the students working on self-study materials. Students are tested again in Week 4. Appendix XI contains evidence about the effectiveness of this strategy. In summary, the average number of prerequisite mathematical skills in which students are not competent at entry is 7.5, and by Week 4 is 1.2. The pass rate on the final test has risen from 58% to 100% over three years, using the same test (see item 12).*

Evidence of the continued study of teaching and learning

22 Record of innovations in teaching

23 Reading of journals and other literature on teaching

24 Teaching qualifications, courses and conferences attended

25 Review of new teaching materials

26 Use of teaching support services

27 Participation in in-house seminars on teaching

28 Participation in course development

29 Pursuit of a line of research which contributes directly to teaching

30 The preparation of a textbook or other instructional material

31 Publication of articles concerned with teaching

32 Contribution to the teaching of one's subject at a national level

33 Involvement in teaching development within your institution

22 Record of innovations in teaching

Description

A list of improvements made to teaching methods and courses, and of new methods adopted.

Rationale

Recurrent attention to small parts of one's teaching and deliberate extension of the repertoire of methods available to a teacher is a useful indication of continuing concern for teaching. As change for change's sake may not be valuable, evidence under this heading may be more convincing if related to evaluation evidence which showed change to be related to the identification of specific problems or possibilities and to have proved successful. The development of variety in teaching methods does not require such justification.

Example

Changes introduced into 997, 998 and 999 since 1985 include:

independent study practicals (see 4)
group project work
reading guides (see 5 and 8)
establishment of resources room (see 6)
office hours for 'drop in' tutorials (see 7)
MCQ tests (see 9 and 10)
tape-slide programmes on methods (see 17)

23 Reading of journals and other literature on teaching

Description

List of journals regularly read or subscribed to, literature owned or studied, and of literature searches undertaken

Rationale

Journals and literature on teaching in higher education, especially those specifically concerned with the teaching of one's subject, can be the source of ideas concerning ways to tackle problems. They can raise the level of sophistication of analysis and provide solution to teaching and learning problems. Specific problems may be attacked with the aid of a proper literature search, just as at the start of a research project.

Example

Regular reader of the ***Times Higher Education Supplement*** *and* ***Journal of Further and Higher Education****. Subscriber to* ***Teaching Egyptology****. I undertook a literature search, and review of available teaching materials, in the area of remedial mathematics for teaching statistics to non-mathematicians (see 21).*

24 Teaching qualifications, courses and conferences attended

Description

Statement of qualification(s) (if any), list of courses attended with indication of their duration, and list of conferences or other special events concerned with teaching.

Rationale

Most lecturers are not qualified to teach and may recognise the need to gain specific expertise by attending short specialist courses. Enthusiastic teachers may attend seminars and conferences provided by one of the many national organisations concerning relevant aspects of their current teaching.

Example

Attendance at a two-week induction course for lecturers at Manchester University; three day course on small-group teaching at the Institute of Education, London University, 1986; attendance at the Annual Conference of SRHE (Society for Research into Higher Education) 1987 and two-day Annual Conference of SCED (Standing Conference on Educational Development) on ***'Course Monitoring and Evaluation'*** *in 1988.*

25 Review of new teaching materials

Description

Brief mention of materials reviewed.

Rationale

This item reflects continued involvement in course development and awareness of new developments. Since most lecturers undertake at least a superficial review of new textbooks as publishers produce them, this item should be limited to more extensive reviews, or those requiring special effort e.g. finding out what computer assisted learning packages exist on a particular topic and trying out a selection of them for their suitability.

Example

I undertook a review of self-study remedial basic mathematics materials (see 21 above); I have selected existing materials for the resources room (4,000+ items catalogued by 01/07/88).

26 Use of teaching support services

Description

Brief mention of services used.

Rationale

Organising and integrating the use of support services (such as the subject librarian, computer services, the educational development service) can take extra effort, initiative and planning, and indicate concern and a greater awareness of possibilities.

Example

Regular use of Educational Methods Unit graphics in the production of OHP transparencies and the design and presentation of materials e.g. reading guides; liaison with subject librarian in stocking of resources room and in production of reading guides; liaison with computer services in use of computer marking of MCQ tests in 999.

27 Participation in in-house seminars on teaching

Description

List of events attended.

Rationale

Enthusiastic teachers may take advantage of opportunities to learn more about teaching, share experiences and widen their repertoire of techniques. Such participation, followed by developments which have been shown to be successful, is evidence of more than simple keenness.

Example

Attendance at Course Evaluation seminar (1986) and Educational Development Service seminar 'Eliciting Student Feedback on Teaching' (1987) which led to use of questionnaires on 997 and 998 (see 17), and running (with Dr P) of two Departmental seminars on course evaluation. These resulted in a Departmental evaluation exercise in 1988 (see 18).

28 Participation in course development

Description

Brief mention of main activities.

Rationale

This is often labelled as an administrative achievement, but may have been undertaken out of concern for teaching, or out of colleagues' recognition of one's teaching excellence, rather than indicating anything about administration. Evidence under this heading may carry special weight when the teacher has been invited to contribute to course development outside the area of his or her own subject specialism.

Example

Jointly responsible for drafting CNAA submission for the Egyptology degree course; member of Faculty Course Review Group 1986– to date; Drafted on to the Library Committee to advise on the establishment of Resource Rooms; Responsible for original design and development of three course units: 997, 998 and 999.

29 Pursuit of a line of research which contributes directly to teaching

Description

Brief mention.

Rationale

While the benefits of research to teaching are invariably claimed they are rarely demonstrated. This is an invitation to demonstrate this relationship.

Example

My primary research interests in the methodology of Egyptology form the basis of unit 999. I have contributed much material to the Resources Room; I invite three visiting speakers a year to the Department. This has resulted in the formation of close personal links with museum research units, which are visited by students on Unit 997 and which have created employment opportunities for 17 students since 1985.

30 The preparation of a textbook or other instructional material

Description

Statement or list, with cross reference to publications list.

Rationale

Whilst normally listed as publications under the heading of research, such achievements may contribute more to, and be better indicators of, teaching excellence.

Example

I am the joint author of ***The New Egyptology*** *(Cairo Press, 1986) which is used as basic text on 997 (item 5 on my publications list). I have produced four tape-slide and two video-tape programmes demonstrating methods (supported by the Teaching Innovations Fund). These are used on 997 and have been sold to four other institutions.*

31 Publication of articles concerned with teaching

Description

Mention or list.

Rationale

Some excellent research and publications are concerned more with the teaching of the subject than with the subject itself. Such publication is rare, and is seldom valued as evidence of research excellence. It may be considered exemplary evidence of teaching excellence.

Example

Teaching Statistics To Egyptology Students *(with Dr W)* ***Egyptology Teaching*** *14, 2, 1-13 1988 (see item 21).*

Resource-based Practicals In Egyptology Paper *presented to the SCED Symposium on resource-based learning, Birmingham Polytechnic, 1988 (see item 5).*

32 Contribution to teaching of one's subject at a national level

Description

Brief mention of activities.

Rationale

Teachers have a responsibility to contribute to scholarship in their subject area. They may also contribute to the teaching of their subject at a national or even international level. Probably only excellent teachers contribute in this way. A very wide range of activities may fall under this heading: editorship of a journal concerned with the teaching of one's subject, membership of a national organisation concerned with the way one's subject develops in schools or higher education, membership of national organisations concerned with teaching and learning, the sponsorship of special events, etc.

Example

Joint sponsor, with Dr D of Hatfield Polytechnic, of SCED Special Conference: ***Developments in the Teaching and Learning of Egyptology*** *held at Hatfield Polytechnic, October 4-6, 1987;*
Sub-editor of the ***Journal of Egyptology*** *in Higher Education;*
Member of the Teaching Methods Working Party of the Society for Research into Higher Education.

33 Involvement in teaching development within your institution

Description

Brief mention of involvement

Rationale

Excellent teachers may be able to contribute to the development of teaching throughout the institution in various ways which indicate concern and the possession of special expertise.

Example

Member of the Educational Methods Committee 1985-88. Contributor of paper to 'Feedback' Course Evaluation seminar on ***Successful Models Of Course Evaluation****. Author of Educational Methods Committee paper (EMC 88/35) on the conflation of exam scores.*